CW0078144Φ

Tolstoy

Tolstoy

In My Own Words

Compiled and edited by
LIZ HORNBY

Hodder & Stoughton
LONDON SYDNEY AUCKLAND

FRONTISPIECE: *Portrait of Tolstoy* by I. Kramskoy
(Tretyakov Gallery, Moscow / Bridgeman Art Library)

Translation copyright © Peter Sekirin

Compilation copyright © Hodder & Stoughton

First published in Great Britain 1999

10 9 8 7 6 5 4 3 2 1

British Library Cataloguing in Publication Data
A record for this book is available from the British Library

ISBN 0 340 73554 6

Typeset in Adobe Goudy Old Style and originated by
Strathmore Publishing Services, London N7

Printed and bound in Great Britain by
Mackays PLC, Chatham, Kent

Hodder and Stoughton Ltd
A Division of Hodder Headline PLC
338 Euston Road
London NW1 3BH

Contents

KNOWLEDGE AND

THOUGHT

'We regret losing a purse
full of money, but squander
good thoughts, which are
infinitely more precious.'

It is better to know a few things which are good and necessary than many things which are useless and mediocre.

No matter how broad humankind's knowledge seems, it is an eternally small part of all possible knowledge.

Knowledge is limitless. Therefore the difference between those who have a little knowledge and those who have more is negligible.

It is not shameful and it is not harmful to be ignorant. Nobody can know everything. But it is shameful and harmful to pretend that you know what you do not.

The importance of knowledge lies in its necessity to work for the goodness and unification of people.

*K*nowledge is a tool and not a purpose in itself.

A clever person cannot be evil. A kind person is always clever. Become kinder by exercising your intellect, and improve your intellect by exercising kindness and love.

*K*nowledge is real knowledge only when it is acquired by the efforts of your thought and not by memory.

*R*ead less, study less, but think more. Learn, both from your teachers and from the books which you read, only those things which you really need and really want to know.

A thought can propel your life in the right direction only when it answers questions asked by your soul. A thought which is borrowed from someone else and then accepted by your mind and memory does not influence your life much and may lead you in the wrong direction.

*E*verything which happens in the lives of human individuals or human societies has had its beginnings in thought. Therefore we can find explanations for everything that has happened to other people not in previous events but in the thoughts which occurred before the event took place.

*I*n order to change the order of things, either in ourselves or in other people, we must change not events, but the thoughts which created the events.

*T*he knowledge which guides your actions is the most precious knowledge.

*Y*ou should think in a good way, and then your thoughts will be turned into good actions. Everything is in our thoughts. Thought is the beginning of everything, and you should guide your thoughts. One of the principal routes to self-perfection lies in guiding your thoughts. If you have misfortunes in your life, look for the cause of this not in your actions, but in the thoughts which inspired you to these actions, and try to improve them. If you are inspired by the events which occur in your life, then look for the origins in your own past thoughts which have caused these events.

*S*ome people live and act according to their own thoughts, and some according to the thoughts of other people. This is one of the major distinctions among people.

A man should use the spiritual heritage which he has received from the wise and holy people of the past, but he should test everything with his intellect, accepting certain things and rejecting others.

A thought which is expressed in the Bible, in the New Testament, in the Koran or in the Indian divine book Upanishad, does not become a truth because it was expressed in a book which is considered to be holy. If we think that every word in every holy book is true, then we are creating an idol. Any important thought, no matter where it comes from, should be discussed; and every thought, no matter who said it, should be given attention.

*W*e should all make use of everything which was created by the united intellect of mankind; and find the proof for everything which was discovered by those who lived before us.

*I*t is bad to irritate people by rejecting their customs and traditions, but it is worse to ignore the demands of your conscience and intellect by following the customs of the crowd.

*D*isrespect for tradition has not caused a thousandth part of the evil that has been caused by observing traditions, customs and institutions that have become meaningless.

*B*efore we can study the central issues of life today, we must destroy the prejudices and fallacies born of previous centuries.

*W*hen you are in company, do not forget your thoughts when you were alone; when you are meditating in solitude, think about what you found out from others.

*N*ature needs small things, but your imagination needs much.

*R*eal knowledge may be obscured by unclear definitions and vague terminology. False scholars create unclear terms and artificial words.

*S*ometimes we are surprised when someone defends illogical thoughts, whether religious, political or intellectual. If he is defending his position with sophisticated reasoning, then you can be sure that reasoning is poor. The decisions of the conscience are always strict and simple.

*T*he purpose of the intellect is to reveal the truth, and therefore it is evil to pervert the truth by means of the intellect.

*U*se the good thoughts of wise people; if you cannot create similar kind and wise thoughts, then at least do not distribute false ones.

*E*very living being has organs which show it its place in the world. For a human being this sense is the intellect. If you do not know your place in the world, the meaning of your life, you should know that there is something at fault – the direction which you have given to your intellect.

*I*t is harmful to eat if you are not hungry. It is even worse to have sex without desire. But the most harmful is to try to think when you do not wish to do so or to try to be engaged in meaningless intellectual activity. Many people do this when they want to improve their position.

*T*here is no worse harm for a person with a strong intellect than giving in to the temptation to make witty remarks and mock his neighbours.

*I*ntellect is the same in everyone and communication is based on intellect, therefore we must all attend to its requirements.

*I*f a person lacks intellect, he cannot distinguish bad from good, and he cannot discern goodness.

*G*od gave his spirit, his intellect, to us, so that we can understand his will and fulfil it. But we have misused it and applied this spirit for the fulfilment of our will.

*T*he more important something is in your life, the more harmful it can be for you to abuse it. People's misfortunes often come from the abuse of that most precious tool of our life: the intellect.

*A*n intellectual life is like a man who carries a lantern in front of him and the lantern lights his way to the last minute. Such a person will never get into a dark place, because the place covered with light moves before him. There is no death in this kind of life because the lantern which is moving before you lights your way, and you follow it as calmly and quietly as you did all your life.

*W*e have misconceptions not because we think illogically but because we live our lives badly.

I understand that the intellect is like a light which shines through translucent glass: I see the light, and I do not know where it comes from, though I know that it exists. We can say the same thing of God.

*T*hose who think constantly about the most important issues of this life can believe that for the human intellect everything is possible.

*W*e are not free in this world; we are imprisoned by our passions and by the emotions of other people to the extent to which we forget the requirements of intellect. If you really want to become free, you can achieve it only by your intellect.

*A*ll that we know, we know through the intellect. And those who do not believe – the people who say that we should not follow our intellect – remind me of those who suggest that we dim the only light that shows the way in the dark.

WISDOM AND TRUTH

'The virtue which is given to us
by wisdom, when compared with
all other knowledge, is as precious as
a vessel filled with water in a desert
when compared with tons of gold.'

There is nothing in which real wisdom cannot be displayed.

There is a natural simplicity, there is the simplicity of wisdom. Both of them evoke love and respect.

The wisdom of this world is to live according to the intellect, even if this way of life may be criticised by others.

The best thing for the development of wisdom is continuous spiritual effort.

A wise person is one who does not consider himself to be wise. And a person never considers himself wise when he has the image of God before him.

*W*isdom is knowledge of good. But we cannot know everything. The real wisdom is not to know everything, but to know what is necessary, what is less necessary, and what is completely unnecessary. Among the necessary knowledge is the knowledge of how to live well – that is, how to produce the least possible evil and the greatest goodness in one's life.

*W*isdom can be achieved by inner work, through solitary communication with yourself; it can also be achieved when you communicate with other people.

*Y*ou should not be upset by seeing wisdom being criticised, as wisdom would not remain real wisdom if it did not reveal the stupidity of a bad life, and people would not be people if they endured this without criticism or without changing their lives.

*T*he more upset a person is with people and circumstances, and the more satisfied he is with himself, the further he is from wisdom.

*W*hen in ancient times people wanted to kill a bear, they hung a heavy log over a bowl of honey. The bear would push the log away in order to eat the honey. The log would swing back and hit the bear. The bear would become irritated and push the log even harder and it would return and hit him more severely. And this would continue until the log killed the bear. People do the same when they return evil for the evil they receive from other people. Could we learn to be wiser than the bear?

*P*eople very often do not accept the truth because they do not like the form in which it is presented to them.

*I*n order that a truth be heard, it is necessary that it be spoken with kindness.

*T*ruth is kind only when it is told by your heart, very sincerely.

*T*o tell the truth is the same as to be a good tailor, or to be a good farmer, or to write beautifully. Any activity needs practice … therefore, in order to tell the truth, you must accustom yourself to doing this. In order to become accustomed to truth, you should tell only the truth, even in small things – in the smallest things.

*I*f truth makes our life easier, it is better to accept truth than to hide it. Our life can be changed, but the truth cannot and will always remain to challenge us.

The real truth is not only a joy but also a weapon in conflict. It is more powerful than violence.

One of the most common mistakes is to think that you can live without truth. The consequences of even the smallest lies are usually more harmful than those small unpleasantnesses which result from telling the truth.

People think that it is no crime to lie to children, that to lie to children is not really very wrong, and even that it is sometimes necessary. But it is clear that with children you should be especially careful and honest.

You should always be truthful, especially to a child. Always do what you have promised, otherwise you will teach the child to lie.

*T*here is no worse misfortune than to be afraid of the truth because it reveals our vices.

*F*reedom cannot be achieved by looking for freedom but in the search for truth.

A man can get used to the worst lies, especially if he sees that everyone around him lives in the same way.

*T*he opinions of a great writer that are accepted by the majority of people can have a deep influence and may be an obstacle to the understanding of real truth.

*D*o not be embarrassed if the notion of God is not clearly expressed to you. The more clearly it is expressed the further it is from its foundation, truth.

The greatest enemy of truth is not a lie but disguising a lie as the truth.

Doubts do not destroy but strengthen the truth.

No one can be completely truthful all the time because different forces and aspirations are fighting within him and sometimes he cannot express them.

Nothing can interfere with the growth of truth – nothing except the wish to preserve old traditions and prejudices.

In order to understand the truth, you should not suppress your intellect. On the contrary, you should purify your intellect, exercise it and intellectually try to test everything which we can possibly put to the test.

A lie can be deliberate if a person knows that he tells a lie and takes some profit from this. At the same time, there are unintentional lies, such as when, in certain circumstances, a person would like to tell the truth, but cannot or does not know how to say it.

WORDS AND ACTIONS

'Let conscience dictate
your words and deeds
whether you are alone
or with others.'

A word is the expression of a thought; thoughts are the expression of divine power. Therefore, words should correspond to that which we mean. Speech can be indifferent, but it should not be an expression of evil.

A person's moral views are reflected in his word.

*W*hen people speak in a smart and sophisticated way, they want to tell a lie or to admire themselves. You should not believe these people. Good speech is always clear, clever and understood by all.

*W*ords unite people; therefore you should speak very clearly and tell only the truth. Nothing unites people more than truth and simplicity.

*I*f you regret once that you did not say something, you will regret a hundred times that you did not remain silent.

*T*hink carefully about what you say – only then will you feel quiet and kind and filled with love. The more irritated you are and the more excited you feel, the more care you must exercise not to sin with your words by abusing others.

*A*s soon as you start criticising someone, stop – especially if you are just repeating gossip.

*T*ime passes, but our words linger for eternity.

*D*o not put your faith in words, either yours or the words of others. Put your faith in the deeds which are performed by you and by others.

*T*o respond to evil with kind words or to do good in return for some evil action is the best and the most accessible way to stop evil in this world.

*O*ne criterion alone distinguishes good deeds from evil ones. If an action leads to love and unity, it is good. If it causes division and animosity, it is evil.

A good life is given only to those who make an effort to achieve it through good deeds, small or large. You should have no less strength or inclination for the smallest acts than for the greatest.

*T*o do a good thing is the only action which definitely gives us bliss. Do not look for an obvious reward for goodness. It is given to you together with your actions.

Do not think that if you do not see the reward for the evil you have done, there will be no response. It already exists in your soul. You are mistaken if you think that the pain which exists in your soul was caused by other reasons.

*T*o sin is as dangerous as to irritate a wild beast. In most cases, evil returns to the evildoer in this world in savage form.

*Y*ou should do goodness without choosing to whom. Good things, once done, will never disappear, even if you forget about them. There is only one sure way to be happy: this is to do goodness and to share this goodness with others.

*T*here is nothing more important than example. It prompts us to do good deeds that would otherwise seem impossible. Therefore if we use dissipated or passionate or cruel people as examples, it destroys our soul. The contrary is also true.

*P*eople are more sensitive to being convinced of ideas in childhood. Meditation and reasoning do not even have one thousandth of the influence which a true example has. Therefore, all teachings about how to behave are funny when children see the opposite in reality.

*I*t is very useful to note the impression which our life and deeds make upon other people.

*M*ost people act not according to meditation and not according to their feelings, but in the light of the senseless repetition of patterns like hypnosis.

*I*f you want to do a good deed, do it now because time will pass and you may not have the chance again.

*W*hen you approach a man, you should think not about how he can help you but how you might serve him.

A good act always requires effort, but when the effort is repeated several times the act becomes a habit.

*T*he more you hurry, the less you can do anything serious.

*L*et plaudits be the consequence of your actions, not their purpose. In order to live only for God, you should do things which no one will ever discover. Do such things, and you will experience a special joy.

Our most important actions are those of which we will never see the consequences.

It is no good hiding your bad deeds, but it is even worse to expose them and be proud of them. To feel shame in the company of other people is good, but it is better to experience shame when you are by yourself. Do not hide anything from other people when they ask you, but do not boast of bad deeds if you are not asked about them.

Not to accept your mistakes means to increase them.

You cannot be completely just. One time you do too little, another time you do too much. There is only one way and that is always to change things, to improve things, to make them better.

*Y*our activity should not be determined by the desires of the people around you but should coincide with the needs of all mankind.

*O*ur deeds become our life, become our fate. This is the law of life.

**UR COMMON**

HUMANITY

'It only seems to us that we are different
from each other. So a flower on a tree
may think that it is a separate being,
but all the flowers are parts of
the blossoming of one apple tree,
and they all come from one seed.'

*I*f at heart we were not all the same, we would never experience compassion for each other.

*E*ven if we do not want to, we can't help but sense our connections with the world of other people; we are connected by industry, by trade, by art, by knowledge and, most important, by the unity of our situation, the common attitude towards life.

*J*ust as one candle lights another and can light thousands of others, so one heart illuminates another heart and can illuminate thousands of others.

*B*eware of destroying the unity of people by stirring up ill feelings among them with your words.

A child meets another child with a smile, displaying friendliness and joy. The same behaviour is displayed by all sincere people. But often a man from one nation, even before he meets a man from another nation, already hates him and is ready to cause him suffering and even death. Those who create these feelings in nations commit a terrible crime.

*P*erfecting the self is both an inner and an outer work. We cannot improve ourselves without communicating with other people and influencing them or being influenced by them.

*W*e should always live as if the most secret corners of our soul were visible to others. Why should we hide things from people? You cannot hide anything from God. All divine and human learning can be summarised in one truth – that we are members of one big family, and we should live our lives in unity, helping each other.

'People should help each other during life,' says the proverb. Without such support people could not survive. Help should be mutual, but this world is created in such a way that some people mostly offer help and others mostly accept it.

We will recognise our limits in this boundless world, and acknowledge our sins, and accept our sins of omission so long as humanity remains human.

Let us forgive each other – only then will we live in peace.

An unfriendly attitude to other people makes life unhappy for everyone. A friendly and loving attitude is oil which lubricates the wheels of life, and makes them move easily and smoothly.

*F*amily and motherland are two segments of the large circle which is humanity. So those who preach morality yet restrict their responsibilities to family and country teach a dangerous selfishness.

*W*e live for ourselves only when we live for others. It seems strange, but try it, and you will discover this truth from your own experience.

*E*verything that unites people is goodness and beauty; whatever separates them is evil. This truth is inscribed on our hearts.

OUR FELLOW

CREATURES

*'We are spiritually connected
on all sides – not only with people
but with all living creatures.'*

*W*e are separate beings, it seems, but in our inner life we are closely connected to all existing living beings. We can feel some of the vibrations of this spiritual world; some of them have not yet reached us, but they are moving as the vibrations of light from the distant stars are moving across the universe; they move though they are not yet visible to our eyes.

*T*he way to understand this world is to understand your inner self. With the help of love and by virtue of the love of others, we understand all beings: people, animals, plants, stones, heavenly bodies. And then again, we understand the attitudes of these beings among themselves; and these attitudes create the whole world as we know it. This way is based on love and on unification with all other creatures in the world.

*T*he idea that we understand ourselves as living beings separate from one another is a consequence of the conditions of our life in time and space. The less we feel this separation, the more we feel unity among ourselves and other living creatures; thereby making our life lighter and more joyful.

*W*hen the suffering of another creature causes you to feel pain, do not flee from the suffering but draw as close as you can and help the one who suffers.

*I*t is strange that societies which support poor children and take care of the animals do not fight for complete vegetarianism when, in most cases, the consumption of meat is the reason for much cruelty.

*T*he killing and eating of animals is willingly accepted by those who think that animals were given to people by God as food and that there is nothing wrong with killing them. It is not true. It may be suggested by some books that it is not a sin to kill an animal, but it is written in our own hearts – more clearly than in any book – that we should take pity on animals in the same way as we do on humans. And, if we do not deaden the voice of our conscience, we all know this.

*I*n our time, the killing of animals for pleasure or food is almost a crime. Hunting and eating meat are not trivial things; they are evil actions, which, like any others, lead to further evil.

*C*ompassion for animals is so natural to us that we can be insensitive to their suffering and death only through tradition or hypnosis.

There is a big difference between someone who has no food except meat and any educated person of our time who lives in a country which has enough vegetables and milk, and who is taught that meat-eating is wrong. The educated person sins greatly if he continues to do that which he knows is wrong.

The better educated people become and the larger our population grows, the more people will turn from eating animals to eating corn and vegetables.

The stupidity, lawlessness and harm, both physical and moral, of meat-eating becomes so clear that meat-eating is supported not by reasoning but by tradition and the practices of the past. Nowadays we should not even debate the issue. It should be self-evident.

LOVE AND KINDNESS

'In relationships, kindness is essential.
If you are not kind to people,
you do not fulfil your
major obligations to them.'

*T*he kinder and more intelligent a person is, the more kindness he can find in other people. Kindness enriches our life; with kindness mysterious things become clear, difficult things become easy and dull things become cheerful.

*L*ove is not the major meaning or source of our life. Love is a consequence, not the source, of everything. The source of our love is the understanding of the divine spiritual beginning which exists in us.

*T*he fearlessness, calm, inner peace and joy which are given to us by love are so fine that nothing in the world can be compared with them, especially for the person who understands the real blessing of love.

*F*or your soul, kindness is the same as health for your body. You do not notice it when you have it.

'I was rewarded with evil for the good I have done,' you cry. But if you love those to whom you do good, you have already received your reward in this feeling of goodness. Therefore all that you do with love, you do for yourself.

If you respond with kindness even to the evil done to you, you will destroy in an evil person that pleasure which he derives from evil. The true teaching of love is strong because it kills evil before the evil grows and becomes powerful.

Those who know the real law are filled with love for others. A test of your love is to love your enemies. Love your enemies, and you will have no enemies.

The most perfect among men is he who loves his neighbour without thinking about whether the person is good or bad.

*E*very time you are wronged, or feel animosity towards someone, remember that all of us are the children of God. Regardless of whether a man is unpleasant to you, you should not stop loving him as your brother because he is God's son.

*P*eople think that there are situations when you can address a person without love. You can work with objects without love – cutting wood, baking bricks, casting iron – but you cannot work with people without love, just as you cannot work with bees without caution. If you are not very cautious with bees, you harm both yourself and the bees. The same happens with people. Mutual love is the highest law of our existence.

*T*hose who say that they love God but dislike their neighbours are lying to others; those who love their neighbours but don't love God are lying to themselves.

*T*he less love a person has, the more he suffers; the more love, the less suffering he has.

If you are in a difficult situation, if you are in a low mood, if you are afraid of other people and of yourself, if you are completely mixed up, then tell yourself: 'I will love everybody I meet in this life,' and try to follow this rule. Then you will see that everything will find its way and everything will be simple, and you will have no doubts or fears.

*L*ove exists only in the present moment. A man who does not manifest love in the present does not love at all.

*A*ll the best qualities of mankind are meaningless and worthless without kindness; even the worst vices can be forgiven with kindness.

*T*here is a natural kindness which comes from our external attributes, from our inheritance, audience, indigestion, success, etc. This kind of kindness is very pleasant, both for the person who experiences it and for the people around him. But it can easily change or be transformed into hatred. And there is another type of kindness which comes from inner, spiritual work. This kindness is less attractive, but it will never disappear and will constantly grow.

*K*indness is the principal quality of the soul. If a person is not kind, it is because he was subjected to some lie, passion or temptation which violated his natural state.

*R*eal love is not just love for some particular person, but the spiritual state of loving everybody.

*I*f you think that it is necessary to judge your neighbour, then say this looking directly into his eyes, and say this in such a way that you do not create animosity.

*H*elping others takes the form both of physical aid and of spiritual support. Stop blaming your neighbour and respect his human dignity.

*L*oving your country and loving your family are good things; however, they can be both a virtue and a vice when they become overwhelming and violate the love for your neighbour.

*A*ssistance given to the poor by the rich is just a polite gesture and not real charity.

Charity is beneficial only when it involves sacrifice because then those who receive the material gift receive a spiritual gift as well.

It is important to teach children kindness and simplicity in life and work. All moral and spiritual education of your children must be supported by your own good example. If you live virtuously, or at least try to do so, then the success of your good life will educate your children.

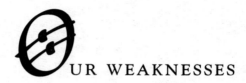

OUR WEAKNESSES

'In the same way as
storms churn the waters,
so too passions trouble our souls
and interfere with our
understanding of this life.'

The more a person follows his intellect and calms down his passions, the closer he comes to the spiritual life and the love of God and of his neighbour.

Seneca, a wise man from Rome, said that when you want to escape from rage, when you feel that your rage is mounting, the best thing is to stop. Do not do anything: do not walk, do not move, do not speak. If your body or your tongue moves at this moment, then the rage will grow.

Rage is harmful to everyone, but it is most harmful to the man who experiences rage.

People are often proud of their control over their desires, and of the force and passion with which they master them. What a strange delusion!

A passion is like a spider's web. At first it is an alien visitor; then it becomes a regular guest; and then it becomes master of the house.

*R*emember how passionately you wanted in the past to have many of the things which you hate or despise now; the same will happen with the desires which excite you at present. Remember how many things you have lost trying to satisfy your former desires: the same thing could happen now. Try to tame your present desires, calm them; this is the most beneficial and the most achievable thing to do.

*O*ne likes blaming other people because it is difficult to restrain oneself from saying things which please one's listeners – that is, blaming other people.

If we saw a man who, instead of covering his house with a roof and putting glass in the window frames, goes out in wet and stormy weather and scolds the wind, the rain and the clouds, we would think that he was insane. But we all do something similar when we are scolding and blaming the evil in other people instead of fighting the evil which exists in ourselves. And it is possible to get rid of the evil inside us, just as it is possible to make a roof and windows for a house. But it is not possible for us to destroy evil in this world, just as we cannot order the weather to change and clouds to disappear. If, instead of teaching others, we would educate and improve ourselves, then there would be less and less evil in this world, and everyone would live a better life.

Stop blaming other people and you will feel what an alcoholic feels when he stops drinking, or what a smoker feels when he stops smoking. You will feel that you have relieved your soul.

*I*f you want to make good your own shortcomings you will never have the time to judge other people.

*T*he more a person is preoccupied with his own personality, the more limited he is; and, on the contrary, the less a person is preoccupied with himself, the stronger he becomes and the more freedom he has.

*O*nly when we forget about ourselves, when we leave behind thoughts of ourselves, can we communicate fruitfully with others, listen to them and influence them.

*E*ating to excess is a regular vice, just as bad as many other vices. We often do not notice it in others because we too are subject to the vice.

*J*ust as a man cannot rise into the air, so he should not praise himself too much. When you praise yourself, you have the opposite effect to the one you desire, and appear lower in the eyes of others.

*I*f you care too much for praise, you will accomplish nothing serious.

*H*e who always listens to what other people say about him will never find inner peace.

*J*ust have a look: what do people in this world think about? They think about everything except the most important things. They think about dancing, music, singing; they think about houses, wealth, power; they are jealous of the wealth of rich people and kings; but they do not think at all about what it is to be human.

*I*f you feel that sometimes, in spite of your desire to subdue your passions, your passions are victorious, do not think that you cannot conquer them. A good groom does not drop the reins when he cannot stop the horses at once, but he perseveres.

*I*f you are living with another person, make an agreement with your partner that as soon as either of you starts to judge the other, you will end the argument.

*W*e often make judgments about other people. We call one person kind, another stupid, the third evil, the fourth clever. But we should not do this. A man changes constantly; he flows like a river, and every day he is different from what he was before. At the very moment you judge him, he changes.

*W*e should be satisfied with the small things in life. And the less we need, the fewer troubles we have.

*I*f you want to find an example to follow, look among simple and humble folk. There is true greatness only in those who do not advertise themselves, who do not regard themselves as great.

*O*nly those who know their own weaknesses can be tolerant of the weaknesses of their neighbours.

*A*lmost always when we look deep into our souls we can find there the very sin that causes us to find fault with others – or something even worse.

*T*here is no worse scoundrel than a man who, when he looks around at other people, can always find an even worse scoundrel than himself and can therefore be quite satisfied with himself.

*C*almness and humility provide pleasures that are not accessible to the selfish and the proud.

*I*f a person is proud, others are puzzled and accord him more importance than he really has; when this influence disappears, he is mocked.

*E*goism in the family can be more cruel than personal egoism and people can do some very unusual things for the reputation of the family.

*P*eople think that self-sacrifice violates our freedom. Those people do not know that self-sacrifice gives us complete freedom and frees us from the slavery of our dissipation.

*T*o repent means to reveal your vices and weakness to all. Repentance is when you take responsibility for your unworthy actions, purify your soul and prepare to accept goodness.

*D*o not hide the shameful memories of your sins in dark corners. On the contrary, keep them close to you, and think of them before you judge your neighbour.

WORK AND IDLENESS

'Work is a necessary condition for happiness: work that is enjoyable and freely undertaken, and physical work that arouses your appetite and afterwards gives you tranquil dreams.'

*I*t seems to us that the most important work in the world is the work which is visible – for example, building a house, ploughing the land, feeding cattle, gathering fruit – and that the work which is invisible – for example, that done by our soul – is not important. But this invisible work on the improvement of our soul is the most important thing in the world.

*P*hysical work as exercise for your body is a necessary condition of life. A man can force others to do things for him, but he cannot free himself from physical work. And if he does not work at necessary and productive things, he will work at unnecessary and stupid things.

*W*ithout exercise of their muscles neither man nor animal can live. So that exercise gives you joy and satisfaction, do some good physical work. This is also one of the best ways of serving others.

*M*anual labour does not exclude intellectual activity; rather, it improves, and even helps, its quality.

*W*ork is a necessity. If you want to be at one with your spirit, work until you are tired – but not so much that you become exhausted. A spiritual frame of mind can be destroyed by idleness as well as by excessive work.

*P*eople often refuse to participate in the innocent joys of life because they claim they are too busy. We should accept moments of recreation because a joyful pastime is sometimes more important than so-called business that would be better left undone, as it is not at all important.

*T*here is the same merit in pleasure as in work. What you do is as important as how you do it.

*T*he creation of this world has been corrupted if rich people can live by the work of the poor yet imagine that they are their benefactors.

*I*f someone is idle, someone else is working overtime. And if someone eats to excess, someone else somewhere is hungry.

MONEY AND POWER

*'Everyone has an equal right
to the privileges of this world.'*

They say that equality is not possible because some people will always be stronger or more intelligent than others. But it is exactly because of this, precisely because some people are stronger and more intelligent than others, said Lichtenberg, that the equality of people is necessary. The advantages of the rich over the poor demonstrate not only inequality of strength and intellect but inequality of civil rights.

Most people are proud not of qualities that command respect but of supremely unimportant, or even harmful, attributes: power and wealth.

The more respect that different objects, customs or laws are accorded, the more attentively we must study the right these things have to our respect.

The earth, the air and the sun belong to all of us and these things cannot belong to anyone.

*I*t is possible to imagine that art could die, but it is not possible to imagine that real art could live, becoming a slave to wealth, laughing at the poor.

*I*t defies the laws of nature for a child to dominate an adult or a fool to guide a wise man. Likewise, it is against the laws of nature for a small group of people to over-indulge while a huge, hungry crowd lacks even the bare necessities.

*W*ealth reminds me of manure in the field. It only makes a bad smell when it is in a large heap; when it is distributed across a field, the smell goes and it makes the soil fertile.

*P*eople strive in this world not for those things which are good, but for what they want to possess and call their property.

The injustice of private property ownership, like any other injustice, is necessarily linked with many other evils, which are used to protect it.

The pleasures of the rich are often acquired through the tears of the poor.

Great wealth does not give satisfaction. As your wealth grows, so do your requirements.

The more a person gives to other people and the less he asks for himself, the better for him. The less he gives to others, and the more he wants for himself, the worse for him.

There are two ways to avoid poverty. The first is to acquire wealth, and the second is to limit your requirements. The first is not always within our power, but the second always is.

For those who live a spiritual life, wealth is not only unnecessary but uncomfortable. It arrests the development of the real life.

VIOLENCE AND WAR

'People of our time try to believe that all
the senselessness and cruelty of life –
with its wealth for the few and poverty
for the majority, with its violence, weapons
and wars – has nothing to do with them,
and they continue to live in the same way.'

No exceptions and no special circumstances can justify the murder of a living person – this is the most vulgar violation of the law of God which is expressed in all religious teaching and in the people's conscience.

The same divine beginning lives in all people, and no single person or gathering of people has the right to destroy the connection between the divine beginning and a human body – that is, to take a human life.

The desire to punish is a very base feeling; it must be suppressed.

The material evil caused by war is large, but it is incomparably small by comparison with the perversion of the understanding of good and evil which happens during war and is inculcated in the souls of people who do not think.

*P*eople think that if they call mass murder 'war', it will cease to be a crime.

*T*he reasons which governments give for wars are always screens, behind which there are completely different reasons and motives.

*T*he misfortunes of, and preparations for, war do not correspond with the reasons given for it: the true reasons are usually so minuscule that they are not even worth discussion, and they are completely unknown to those who die.

*W*ar creates a state in which the power and glory are often received at the end by the most undeserving and vicious people.

*W*hat purpose does a man's intellect serve if you are going to influence him only with violence?

*S*tate violence cannot be destroyed by decrees, but only by truth and love. Maybe state violence was necessary for previous generations of people; maybe it is necessary even now; but people should visualise and encourage for the future the kind of government where violence will not be necessary for the peaceful existence of people.

*W*ar can be destroyed only if people stop participating in violence and are ready to be persecuted for not participating in this violence. This is the only way to stop war.

*P*eople are clever beings and they can live according to their intellect; and sooner or later they will change violence into complete harmony and understanding. Yet every act of violence makes this time more distant from today.

OUR PATH

THROUGH LIFE

*'We cannot reach complete
understanding of the meaning of life.
We can only discover its direction.'*

*E*verywhere on earth you are equally close to heaven, to limitless eternity. The real way of life is very narrow, but it is important to find it. You will understand it easily, as we understand a path which is made of pieces of wood put across a swamp. If you step aside from them, you will get sucked into the swamp of misunderstanding and evil. A clever man returns to the true path at once, but a foolish man goes further and further into the swamp, and then it becomes more and more difficult for him to get out.

*I*n order to move, you must know the direction in which to go. The same should happen with your life if you are to lead a clever and good life. You should know where life leads both you and other people.

*W*e know our life only as it exists here, in this world; if our life has any meaning, it should be evident to us here.

*R*eal life is only in the present. If people tell you that you should live this life preparing for the future, do not believe them. We live in this life, and we know this life only, so all your efforts should be directed towards the improvement of this life.

*W*e make our decisions in the present, and the present exists out of time; it is a tiny moment where two periods meet – the past and the future. Therefore, during the present a person is always free to make his choice.

*J*ust imagine to yourself that the purpose of your life is your happiness only – and then life becomes a cruel and senseless thing. You have to embrace what the wisdom of humanity, your intellect and your heart all tell you – that the meaning of life is to serve the divine will which sent you into this world; then life will become a constant joy.

The best way to live joyfully is to believe that life was given for joy. When joy disappears look for your mistake.

Without a clear understanding of the meaning of our life, without the thing that we call faith, we can suddenly deny the things for the sake of which we live, and start to live for those things which we hate.

We all know that we do not live the right way, the way that we should. If you concede that your life ought to be better, you must never forget this. Stop complaining about contemporary life; be willing to improve it. We must all believe that real life should be better than contemporary life and should live in such a way that life improves.

*Y*ou cannot improve yourself, you cannot become perfect, if you live with the concerns of everyday life. Yet it is least possible if you live in solitude all the time. The best means of improving yourself is to work at yourself in solitude, increasing your understanding and clarifying your view of the world, and then, being amongst people again, apply this to your life and actions.

A person can fulfil his purpose in life as well in illness as in good health.

*I*t might seem that it would be impossible to live without discovering a purpose to your life. In spite of this, most people who consider themselves educated are proud that they have reached some height in life from which it seems to them that life has no meaning.

*P*eople can understand their real destination in life only after they free themselves from this sensual, material world.

*L*ife is constant change; it consists in weakening the material and increasing the spiritual side of our existence.

A sailor who sails close to the shore can get his bearings from the shoreline or cliffs. But when sailors go far out to sea, they have only the stars in the sky to guide them and the compass to indicate their direction. These are given to us.

*T*he most necessary expression of freedom is to give your thoughts a specific direction.

*W*e hear often that there is no profit in improving our life, combating evil or fighting for justice because progress will occur by itself. This is as likely as a journey successfully completed on board a rudderless ship.

*T*here are no guides more false than the opinions of other people.

*I*n the long run, people achieve only those things which they set as goals for themselves; and therefore, you should set the highest possible goals for yourself.

*M*ankind moves ceaselessly towards perfection, not of its own accord but through the efforts of certain people who seek their personal perfection. The kingdom of God will be created by their efforts.

*P*ursue the principal purpose of your life, tending your own soul, and be confident that only in this way will you contribute to the improvement of society.

*I*f you see that some aspects of society are bad, and you want to improve this world, there is only one way to do it: you have to improve people. And in order to improve people, you can do only one thing; you must become better yourself.

*I*n this world we are like a child who enters a room where someone wise is speaking. The child has not heard the beginning, and he leaves before the end of the speech; there are certain things he has heard but does not understand. In the same way, the great speech of God began many centuries before we started learning, and it will continue for many centuries after we disappear and turn to dust. We have heard only part of it, and we have not understood most of what we have heard; nevertheless, a bit vaguely, we have understood something great, something important.

95

*L*ife is not given to us that we might live idly without work. No, our life is a struggle and a journey. Good must struggle with evil; truth must struggle with falsehood; freedom must struggle with slavery; love must struggle with dissipation. Life is movement, and we walk along the path of life in accordance with ideas which illuminate both our intellect and our heart with divine light.

*W*e suffer from the past, and we spoil our future because we neglect the present.

FAITH AND RELIGION

'Humanity has never lived,
and could not live,
without religion.'

The essence of every religion is to answer the question, 'Why do I live, and what is my attitude to the limitless world which surrounds me?' There is not a single religion, from the most sophisticated to the most primitive, which does not have as its basis the definition of this attitude of a person to the world.

Faith is the understanding of the meaning of life and the acceptance of your duties and responsibilities connected with it.

Do not think that you can find peace for your soul without faith.

The greatest insolence is the establishment by some of a religious law which is to be accepted by all others without discussion or question. Why must people do this?

*T*here are some who assume responsibility for making decisions for others and determining their relationship with God and with the world, and there are others, the overwhelming majority, who give this authority to the others and blindly believe everything that they are told. Both groups of people commit an equal crime.

*W*e should not replace real religious progress with other progress – technical, scholarly and artistic. Technical, scholarly and artistic achievements can coexist with religious backwardness, as happens in our time.

*T*o pray means to accept and to remember the laws of the limitless being, God, and to measure all your deeds in the past and in the future according to his laws. And it is useful to do this as often as possible.

*B*efore you start praying determine for yourself whether you can concentrate; otherwise do not pray at all.

*P*ersonality is a limitation; therefore God, as we understand him, has no personality. Prayer is our address to God. How can we address someone who has no personality? I address God as if he were a person, though I know that he is not.

*T*he more closely a person unites with the will of God, the firmer he becomes in his actions. A traveller planning a journey along a road threatened by robbers, does not travel alone. He looks for a friend, someone who can be his escort. And then he follows the escort, protected from the robbers. A clever man behaves in the same way in his life: 'There are so many troubles in this world. How can I stand all this? What friend or escort will I find so that I can pass this way without fear? To whom should I turn?' There is only one real friend: this is God.

*I*t is a mistake to think that faith will remain the same for all time. The longer people live, the clearer, simpler and stronger their faith becomes. And the clearer, simpler and stronger their faith becomes, the better people live.

If you believe that faith cannot be changed, you might as well think that the fairytales your grandmother told you when you were a little child are true, and that you will believe them for the whole of your life.

*T*he stronger our faith, the better we understand what is and what should be the guide of all our actions.

*H*e who is not afraid of anything, and is ready to give his life for the true cause, is much stronger than he whom other people fear and who has the lives of others in his power.

*T*he greatest joy, according to the works of St Francis of Assisi, is that you can endure everything. You may suffer slander or physical pain, yet in the end you are able to feel no animosity, but only joy, because you have faith. Such joy cannot be destroyed either by evil people or by your own suffering.

*I*n our world, real faith in most cases is substituted by public opinion. People do not believe in God, but they believe in many minor things which are taught by other people.

*T*here are people who think that they do not have faith. This is not true. They only do not know their true faith, or do not want it, or cannot express it when they have it.

*R*eal faith does not need any outer support; it does not need the outer glamour; it does not need to be forcibly induced. God has a great deal of time, and thousands of years pass as one. Those who want to support their faith with violence and force, in order to distribute it faster, either do not believe themselves, or believe very little.

*I*f you know that you do not have faith, you should know that you are in one of the most dangerous situations in which a person can be in this world.

*F*aith in the existence of eternity is the quality of humanity.

What we should teach our children are those things which are common to all religions – Buddhist, Muslim, Christian, Jewish, etc., and those things which are clear to everybody: the moral science of love and the unification of people.

Most people do not listen to God, but adore him. It would be better not to adore but to listen.

At the moment when the members of a religious gathering said, 'The Holy Spirit is among us,' when they claimed the highest authority and considered the results of their own meditation as more profound than the divine beginning that exists in everyone (that is, the intellect and the conscience) – at that moment a great lie was born. It still traduces the bodies and souls of many people, has destroyed millions of human beings and continues its terrible work.

*F*aith answers those questions to which the intellect cannot find the solutions.

*O*nly religion destroys egoism and selfishness, so that one starts to live life not only for oneself. Only religion destroys the fear of death; only religion gives us the meaning of life; only religion creates equality among people; only religion sets a person free from outer pressures. We must believe those spiritual doctrines which provide a very simple and practical guide for every one of us.

LIFE AND DEATH

'There is something in the soul which
cannot die, or which cannot be affected
by death. Sometimes we can understand
this, and sometimes we cannot.'

When a person leads a good life, he is happy in the present moment and he does not think what will happen after this life. If he remembers about death, then, looking at how well this life is organised, he believes that after death everything will be as good as it is now. It is much better to believe that everything which God makes for us is good than to believe in all the pleasures of paradise.

If one is a material being, then death is the end of everything. But if one is a spiritual being, then the body limits one's spiritual being, and death is only a change.

Only those who do not believe in eternity have never seriously considered death.

The more spiritual a life we lead the less afraid of death we are. If a person lives a spiritual life, then he is not afraid of death. Death for such a person means setting his spirit free from his body. And he knows that the things with which he lives cannot be destroyed.

Death is the destruction of this body with which I understand the world in this life, and the destruction of the glass through which I look at the world. And we do not know whether this glass will be replaced by another, or whether the essence which looks through the window will integrate with the world.

The fear of death is not characteristic of all living beings. In a man, the fear of death is the acknowledgement of his sins.

You should live your life so that you are not afraid of death and at the same time do not wish to die.

*P*ain is a necessary condition of the body just as suffering is the necessary condition of our spiritual life, from birth to death.

*L*ife is a constant approach to death and therefore life can be bliss only when death does not seem to be an evil.

*E*veryone should decide questions of life and death for himself.

*A*t the time of our death, we can see a candle by the light of which we read the book of a life filled with problems, lies, evils and misfortunes. And in the moments of death, this candle illuminates the whole world, and all the corners of a person's life, very brightly and clearly – even those corners which have always been hidden in darkness. Then the light gutters, and dims, and disappears for ever.

*W*hen you prepare yourself for death, do not worry about the usual things. Prepare to die in the best way possible. Take advantage of the power of the moment of death, when a person exists partially in the other world, and his words and deeds have special power over those who remain in this one.

*W*e die alone, as we live our spiritual life alone.

*I*f we believe that everything that happens to us in this life happens for our good (and every religious person should believe this), then we must believe that everything that happens to us when we die also happens for our good.

THE SPIRITUAL LIFE

'A person can understand himself as
a material or a spiritual being.
When you understand yourself as
a spiritual being, then you are free.
For a material person there is not even
the slightest question of being free.'

*W*e have only one sinless guide, the universal spirit which gets into all of us though we are all individuals, and which gives us all the urge to do all the things which are necessary. The same spirit which exists in a tree and pushes it to grow straight and to produce seeds exists in us, urges us to be closer to God and brings us closer to each other.

*L*ive in God; live together with God by understanding him in you; do not try to define him with words.

*O*nly those things which are unseen and which cannot be tasted, those things which are spiritual, which are understood in ourselves, only those things are real. The things which can be seen and felt are the creations of our feelings and therefore they are an illusion.

A man asks God or other people for help, but only his good life can help him. And this you can do on your own.

A person who accepts the divinity of his soul and lives with it has everything he can possibly wish for his own good.

*P*eople who deny freedom are like a blind man who denies the existence of colours. They do not know the nature of freedom.

*T*he greatest changes in the world are made slowly and gradually, not through eruptions and revolutions. The same is true of one's spiritual life.

*T*ake from someone who follows the divine law everything which other people think represents comfort and wealth, and he will remain happy.

We have a law for all our actions, and it cannot be restricted by any power. Obedience to the law is possible even in prison and under the threat of torture and death.

We may not be able to see the usefulness of moral suffering, but that suffering makes us better and draws us closer to God.

When you suffer, do not think of escaping, but concentrate your efforts on the inner spiritual strength this suffering requires.

They are mistaken, those who think that they can live the high spiritual life but whose bodies are filled with idleness and luxury.

*T*his world is not a place for crying, not a trial, but something unimaginable. The joy of life could be endless if we were only to enjoy it properly, as it was given to us.

*T*he essence of life lies not in your body but in your conscience.

*I*llness almost always destroys physical power, but it releases the power of the soul. For a person who concentrates his consciousness in the spiritual domain, illness does not diminish his goodness, but on the contrary increases it.

*E*very person has a depth to his inner life, and its essence cannot be explained. Sometimes you want to explain it to people, but then you see that it is not possible to explain this to any other person. Hence you must have your own channel of communication with God. Do not seek anything else.

A fruitful prayer is the establishment in your conscious mind of the understanding of life's meaning and you can experience this state during the best minutes of your life.

A person who knows all sciences but does not know himself is a poor and ignorant person. He who does not know anything except for his inner spiritual self is an enlightened person.

*I*f you could only know who you are, all your troubles would seem utterly unnecessary and trivial.

A child preserves his soul as an eyelid protects the eye; and without the keys of love he lets no one enter his soul.

*W*hat time could be better than childhood, and what virtues could be better than innocent joyfulness, and the necessity of love? They are the only real manifestations of life. You should respect every person, but you should respect a child a hundred times more than any person, and not destroy the innocent purity of this soul.

A person would cry from pain if, after a period of idleness, he started to do hard physical work. In the same way, the man who works on the improvement of his spiritual world has many pains caused by different misfortunes, which other people do not notice.

*T*emporary solitude from all things in this life, and meditation within yourself about the divine, is spiritual good as necessary for your soul as material food is for your body.

*T*hose who get to know themselves will discover good.

Only he who understands himself as a spiritual being can understand the spiritual dignity of others.

Terrible is the situation of those who cannot perceive spiritual growth in themselves. They can see only physical life which will disappear in time. When you understand your spiritual being and live with it, then instead of despair you will understand the joy which can never be destroyed and which always grows.

Under my feet there is frozen earth; around me stand huge trees; above my head is the cold, foggy sky; I am aware of my body and that I am busy with thoughts. I know that all these things – the earth, the trees, the sky, my body, my thoughts – have been created by chance, that this is a temporary world, and that it is the creation of my five senses. Yet I know that when I die, which I will, the world of which I am now part will not disappear.